Hope
through
Heartsongs

Other books written and illustrated by
Mattie J.T. Stepanek

Heartsongs

Journey Through Heartsongs

Hope through Heartsongs

Written and Illustrated

by

Mattie J.T. Stepanek

Poet & Peacemaker

 HYPERION

NEW YORK

ISBN: 0-7868-6944-5

Hyperion books are available for special promotions and premiums.
For details contact Hyperion Special Markets, 77 West 66th Street, 11th floor,
New York, New York, 10023, or call 212-456-0100.

10 9 8 7 6 5 4 3 2 1

This book is dedicated to *all* people
who are struggling to find hope...
especially the children of our world and their families.
Remember to play after every storm!

—Love, Mattie

Acknowledgments

Thank you to VSP Books for first making me a published "poet and peace-maker," and to Hyperion for helping me spread the message of my heartsongs in a huge way.

Thank you to the Muscular Dystrophy Association, Children's National Medical Center, and Children's Hospice International for giving me the chance to live, and to love life while I am living it.

Thank you to Oprah Winfrey and Jimmy Carter for giving me hope, and for teaching kids and other people that they can be real friends with real-life heroes.

Thank you to Jerry Lewis, Ed McMahon, Chris Cuomo, Laura Bush, Gary Zukav, Bernie Siegel, Harold Schaitberger, Mia Hamm, and Mike Myers for letting me talk with the "famous people" and learn that they are seeking hope just like everyone else.

Thank you to Sandy, Lyn, Mike, Valerie, Mollie, Teresa, Candie, Leslie, D.J., Tom, Brian, Libby, Shelly, Kelly, "J.K.," Amy, the Firefighters, the Harley folks, the D'Anna family, Dr. Kim, Dr. Fink, Laura, Rita, Regina, Peggy, Terry, Marissa, Cynda, Bob, Mary Ellen, Bob, Deneen, Patricia, Judy, all of my teachers, and most of all, my mom, for protecting and supporting me, and for helping me trust in grown-ups to hear and meet the needs of children.

Thank you to Nick, Ben, Hope, and Marie, and to Hedder, Jamie-D., Chris, Arlo, Kunpal, Jessie, Kenny, Jimmy, Tommy, Amanda, Heather, David, Daniel, Ryan, Erin, Neil, Sarah, Will, Alex, Kristen, and Guder for letting me grow and be with some of the best kin and friends in the world.

Love, Mattie

Foreword

In the past, most of us were born limited to the perceptions of the five senses. From this perspective, the entire universe consists of what we can see, smell, hear, taste, and touch. Each of us is a body and a mind, but no more. A relative few of us were born able to see beyond the five senses. From this perspective, each individual is much more than a body and a mind, and, in addition, is an immortal soul. For such individuals, the five senses do not disappear, but another sensory capability is active. That is the perception of the soul.

The perception of the soul is multisensory perception. Multisensory perception is now emerging in millions of humans. They see meaning in everyday circumstances. They yearn for meaning more than for security and comfort, and even more than wealth, fame, and success. They long for the needs of their souls—harmony, cooperation, sharing, and reverence for Life.

As multisensory perception emerges throughout the human family, the human experience appears as more than a journey from birth to death. It appears also as a chapter in a larger book with a multitude of chapters. Each chapter is a life in the Earth school—the learning environment of the five senses—and the book is the chronicle of a soul as it enters the Earth school again and again to learn and to contribute.

Chapters begin and end, but the book continues. Five-sensory humans mistake their lives for the book. A multisensory human sees his life as a chapter in the book. He sees the lives of others in the same way. A multisensory human does not think of herself as beginning with her birth or ending with her death any more than she thinks that a book ends when one of its chapters comes to conclusion. The unfolding history of the book becomes more and more visible in each chapter—in each life.

This is apparent when a young person sees, thinks, speaks, acts, and feels with wisdom that a few years in the Earth school cannot explain. Mattie Stepanek was eleven years old when I first spoke with him, yet he spoke to me of peace, humility, and gratitude. He spoke of giving gifts that would benefit others even after he died. He spoke of heavenly Angels and angels that are even more important to him—everyday Angels. You and I are everyday Angels when we are kind to each other, listen to each other, care about each other, and help each other. He also spoke of messages from his heart, which he called heartsongs. His desire was to be a peace-maker and, through his poetry, create peace and help others discover their heartsongs and listen to them.

When you desire the same things, you tap into the accumulating wisdom of the book in which you are a chapter. Then you become an inspiration to others in the same way that Mattie is an inspiration to us. We are each Angels-in-the-making, and that is why we can see and honor in others, such as Mattie, the goal that each of us is traveling toward. Mattie reminds us of that goal and makes us thankful.

—Gary Zukav

Introduction

Hello everybody. This is Matthew Joseph Thaddeus Stepanek, but I prefer to be called Mattie. Welcome to *Hope Through Heartsongs*, my third book to be published. The words that fill these pages are created and joined in the form of poetry. Therefore, it will be considered a work of fiction, like first my two books, *Heartsongs* and *Journey Through Heartsongs*. But I want to tell you this: the message of this book is not fiction…it is true.

My poetry comes from my heart and from my life. I have been creating poetry about my feelings, my happiness, my pain, my dreams, my fears, my insights, and more, since I was three years old. These passages speak about my experiences with disability, death, and divorce, and they speak about the possibilities of strength, future, and peace. Sometimes, a poem just comes to me, and I can't type fast enough to keep up with my thoughts. Sometimes, an idea comes to me that will become a poem, but I just capture a thought and write the poem later (sometimes months or even years later). And sometimes, a poem is a part of a school assignment, or is born from an essay or journal entry I have written at some time. But at all times, my poetry is a part of my heartsong, whether the reality of the message is sad or serious or silly or significant.

I first began using the term "heartsong" when I was about five years old. I was creating some poetry, and happened to be wearing a sweatshirt with a little music-maker inside the fabric. I leaned against something while I was making my poetry, and the music began. I whispered, "Mommy, listen, that's my heartsong." And I immediately wrote a poem, called "Heartsong," that told all about it. I call it my "master poem," and included it in my first books to help people understand.

A heartsong is something deep inside each of us. It's our sense of why we are here and how we can keep going. It is like a purpose. It may be to live as a mommy or a daddy, or a firefighter or a delivery person, or a child with a disability who teaches others about patience and love and acceptance. Heartsongs are usually easy to hear when we are young, but we sometimes get too busy or hurt or angry to listen to them as we get older. And just like any gift that isn't cared for or used well, it is possible to forget how to listen to the message of each song. But even if we completely lose our heartsong, we can share someone else's song until we are able to reawaken or recreate our own.

The message of the heartsongs that I am sharing in this book is hope. Hope is essential to our lives each day. With hope, we can optimistically anticipate our future, rather than merely awaiting it, or allowing it, to occur. Hope brings brightness to each point of view, and a confident desire to be proactive and enthusiastic in meeting challenges and in overcoming obstacles. It is important to know, however, that to have hope, we must also explore the feelings and realities that come with our struggles—personal struggles, struggles with other people, and struggles with events that take place around our world.

It would be easy for each of us to stay shocked, angry, hurt, or sad with all the difficult things that we face in life. And even though it is difficult and sometimes almost overwhelming to examine feelings related to loss and loneliness and alarming turmoil, it is the only way that we can grow, individually and together. We cannot let sad or traumatic events, or even acts of terror, be the death of hope. That is why this book explores these issues, and finds that in spite of each struggle, we can and will find hope if we choose to do so.

If I could offer each person a wish for being, it would be a spirit of understanding and faith. If I could offer all people a wish for being with each other, it would be a spirit of acceptance and forgiveness. And if I could offer our world a wish, it would be a spirit of peace, so that we can *be*, together. My prayer now is that by sharing my heartsongs, their message may offer a spirit of hope, which may inspire the courage needed for people to make the choice and accept the offers of all of these wishes. Thank you for sharing my heartsongs with me, and with others.

Love,
Mattie

Contents

Hope
for
Within

Choice Lesson

Growth brings change.
Unpredictable change,
Which can bring
Hesitancy to optimism.
It is essential that we cope
With the realities of the past
And the uncertainties of the future
With a pure and chosen hope.
Not a blind faith,
But a strengthened choice.
Then, we can have the
Fortitude and wisdom necessary
To integrate life's many lessons
That collect beyond points in time.
Growing like this will help
Build a good future,
For individuals,
For communities,
And for the world.

February 2000

Birth-Tears

When I was a little
Teeny-tiny baby
And I came out of
My mommy's womb,
I cried.
That's what most babies
Do when they are born.
Do you know why
I cried when I was born?
I cried for the same
Reason that most babies
Cry when they are born.
I cried because I was so happy.
I cried because I got to come
And live in this family.
I cried because God was
So good to let me have
The best mommy in the world.
And that is why most
Babies cry when they are born...
They are happy birth-tears
Because we are so happy
To be in the best families.

June 1996

About Normal

Right now,
I don't know what Normal is
Anymore.
That's because Normal has been changing
So much,
So often,
Lately.
For a long while of lately.
I'd like Normal to be
Okayness.
Good health…
Emotional health,
Medical health,
Spiritual health.
I'd like Normal to be
Like that.
I'd like Normal to stay,
Like that.
For now though,
I know that Normal won't be normal
For a little while…
But somehow,
Sometime,
Even if things are not Normal,
They'll be okay.
That's because I believe
In the great scheme of things,
And Life.

May 2001

5

It Happened Anyway

When Jamie died,
And I didn't even understand
The eternity of my sadness,
I wished I could have prevented it.
But then, I remember,
It happened anyway.
When I rest in my bed,
And dream about how I could have
Lived and played with my brother,
I wish I could have stopped his death.
But then, I remember,
It happened anyway.
When I look at pictures,
And imagine what he would be like
Now a dozen years old,
I wish I could have saved him from agelessness.
But then, I remember,
It happened anyway.
When I hug our mommy,
And we think of why, and how, and
When he was with us and left us,
We wish we could have prevented it,
And stopped his death, and saved him from
Never needing breath for birthday candles...
But then, we remember, though we don't understand,
It happened anyway.

November 2001

6

Dear God,

I've been having these dreams,
That make me think that it is real,
And that it will really happen.
Like about a monster taking me away from
Home without anything to take with me and
I never see my mother again.
Dear God,
Please help me have some special medicine
That will get rid of all these nightmares
About going away, and leaving, and dying.
Dear God,
I will thank You for the special medicine,
Even if it's invisible medicine that is
Inside of all the healthy food I eat everyday,
Or inside of all the meditation I do everyday.
Dear God,
I send You big hugs and big kisses, and
You will send me the invisible medicine
To cure this scariness and
To get over these feelings and nightmares.
Please put it into all of the food that I eat
So they won't come ever again,
Even while I am still getting better.
I need to get rid of this tiredness in my heart.
Amen.

August 1996

Land of Loneliness

Sometimes,
I feel like I have
Broken through
The wall into the
Land of Loneliness.
I cry in my mind, and
I cry in my heart, but
I never cry in my eyes.
I don't want anyone
To know how
Sad and how
Lonely and how
Different I feel.
I know that I don't
Always feel this way,
But I feel this way now.
I don't like feeling this
Way now, or any-ever.

April 1996

Shared Tears

Sometimes,
I get sad,
And then
I have tears
On my face.
They roll
Out of my eyes,
Down onto my cheeks,
And off of my chin.
Sometimes,
My mommy
Takes one of my tears
On her finger,
And kisses it,
And puts it
Onto her face.
My mommy loves me.
When I am
Hurt or very sad,
My mommy is
Hurt or very sad, too.

October 1993

9

Reality

Sometimes,
I really miss
Having a brother.
I miss my
Two brothers and my sister,
And I don't
Understand
Why they died.
Sometimes,
It's so sad
To not have
A brother, and
Another brother, and
A sister
When I should have them.
And I know that
Something
Will make me
Happy again.
But, right now,
I don't know what, and
I don't know when.

January 1995

Little Boy Blue

Sometimes,
I am very, very, very sad.
And I don't know why.
But I know I am
Alone with my tears.
I am not angry,
But I am so sad.
I miss Jamie.
I want him to come back,
So I can touch him again.
Sometimes,
My mommy and my Mr. Bunny
Touch my tears.
They hold me and rock me,
And love my tears away,
Out of my eyes,
And off of my cheeks.
I am still sad then,
And I still miss Jamie,
But sometimes,
I am a little bit happier.

November 1993

At Mommy's Work

Today I went to my mommy's work with her.
I played with my work-friends,
Emily and Andrew.
Their mommies work, too.
We ate in a restaurant,
And I let my lunch balloon
Go up to the sky
And into Heaven for my brother, Jamie.
I ran and ran with my work-friends,
And then my heart hurt
Next to my belly-button
And I asked Mommy
To put on my oxygen-wind.
I was sad and tired and hurt.
But then the little boy work-friend
Covered his head with rubberbands.
He covered his ears and his nose, too,
He covered the floor and even the hall.
It was so silly of him.
And I laughed and laughed and laughed.
I was not sad anymore.
Then his mommy told him to clean up,
And he was not silly anymore,
So I did not laugh anymore.
But in the car going home,
I fell asleep,
And when I woke up,
I remembered my silly work-friend,
And I laughed and laughed
And laughed again.

December 1993

a-byss'

My life
Is halfway down
An abyss.
A deep
Immeasurable space.
A gulf.
A cavity.
A vast chasm.
My life
Is not how
I planned it to be.
Is not how
I want it to be.
Is not how
I pray for it
To be.
In the darkness
Of this pit,
I see a small
Light of hope.

Is it possible for me
To climb to such heights?
To rebuild the bridges?
To find my salvation?
The song
In my heart
Is so quiet.
Is so dark.
Is so fearful.
I dare not stay in
This abyss.
Though deep
And vast,
I am only halfway
Down.
Thus, I am
Already
Halfway up?
Let such words
Fall onto my heart,
And raise me from this depth.

January 2001

14

Bravery Prayer

Dear God,
Help us to always be able
To use the feelings of
Hope and fear, together,
In one great force...
Bravery.
Bravery is extremely
Necessary in life.
If we are able
To have bravery,
We will be able
To achieve
Many goals in life.
Amen.

December 1999

15

Life: That's Amazing!

When it is nighttime,
I get my nebulizer and All my medicines,
I go to the bathroom and brush my teeth,
I put on my pajamas and heart monitor,
And untangle my oxygen-mustache
So I get my special breathing wind.
When I am in my bed,
My mommy will read me a book,
And say my prayers with me.
She will kiss me and hug me and tuck me in,
And then turn on my Mommy-Songs tape.
When I close my eyes,
I go to sleep and dream and dream,
Or I go to sleep and do not dream.
When it is morning,
I wake up.
I am alive, and
I am breathing, and
I am a real boy.
That's Amazing!

October 1993

Morning Alarm

When I wake up
In the morning
After a night
When I have
A lot of alarms
For not breathing and
For low heart rate,
I forget so many things.
I cannot concentrate.
I am impatient.
And even though
It all gets better as
The day goes on,
I feel like I have
Young person's
Al Simer's disease.

April 2000

Beyond the Pain

I am looking out of the window.
I see so many beautiful things.
I see trucks and cars,
And flowers and plants,
And people.
I like looking out of the window.
People are such beautiful things.

September 1993

Hope
for
Each Other

Fair Feelings

Everyone has feelings—
Love, fear, sadness,
Happiness, confusion, hope...
Feelings depend on one's
Personal situation at a given time.
We should feel free and
Encouraged to express feelings,
But never in a way
That hurts the feelings of others.
Even if a person does not think
It is a big deal to say something
That could upset another person,
It could be a very crushing
Experience to that person.
It could affect the rest
Of his or her life, and
Possibly, even the lives of others
Subsequently touched by that person.
Attitudes are contagious.

March 2000

About Feelings

Some things hurt my feelings.
Like when other people tease me.
I have been teased by kids
About my oxygen, and
About not being able to keep up.
I have been teased by kids
For not teasing other kids,
And for setting a moral example.
I have been teased by someone
For not keeping scary secrets, and
For being afraid of threatening things.
I have even been teased by someone
About having a disability.
When things have hurt my feelings,
Usually I try to talk
To the person who has hurt me.
Sometimes, I have to talk
To a person I trust instead.
It is important for people to be
Honest when expressing themselves.
But, it is also important to be
Always thoughtful and considerate
In expressing feelings to others,
So that more feelings are not hurt.

                              March 2000

22

On Saying "Good-bye"

There are too many
Good-byes in my life.
Just too many,
Too many,
Too many good-byes.
Things were so sad,
And then,
Things were so bad,
And now,
Things are so much better,
But, I have to say
"Good-bye"—
And even though there
Will be another "hello,"
I don't want to see the
Friends and times of this
Best-of-all-summers go.
And if only my friends
Could be with me a
Little longer,
Just one more week—
I'd have seven more
Whole days
Before I'd have to cry.

July 1998

23

Lunch Hour

This was really not a very good day.
I played with my friend, Lissa,
And we began to argue
And hit at each other.
At first, I thought it felt good
  because
That's what Lissa does with her
  sister.
When they argue, they hit at each
  other.
So when I hit at Lissa,
I thought maybe it would be
Just like if my sister, Katie,
Was still alive and we were
  arguing.
But it didn't really feel good.
And when I told Mommy about it,
She was disappointed that I hit.
She said we touch gently in our
  family.
She said if Katie was alive,
We would probably argue,
But hitting would not be okay.

Mommy told me to sit and think
About how to disagree, but not
  hurt.
Then I knew it was not a very
  good day.
I tried to think about why I hit
  Lissa.
I don't want to be mean.
I don't always have to get my way.
I don't think I am a bad boy.
So I think that perhaps I hit Lissa
Because God went out to lunch,
And he could not come into my
  heart
And remind me to be peaceful
  when I was angry.
I sure hope God doesn't go out
  often.

January 1996

24

Examination of Faith (II)

Dear God,
When Mommy told me that
The little baby growing in Margie
Died last night,
I was surprised and angry.
I prayed to You, God.
I prayed every night and
I prayed every day and
We all prayed that this
Sweet little baby would live.
When Mommy told me that
The baby died, I said,
"Then our prayers didn't work!
God didn't listen! God didn't
Make a miracle for the baby!"
Mommy said that You
Always listen to our prayers,
But sometimes Your answer
Is not what we were wishing for,
And "prayers" are not "wishes."
She said that maybe letting
The baby come into Heaven
As such a tiny angel was a
    miracle.
There are miracles every single day
Except we don't always notice them,
Because we were hoping or
    wanting for
Something different than what
    we got.
So God,
Thank You for all the miracles
You give to us each day,
And thank You for listening
To *all* of our prayers.
And even though I am sad about
Margie's baby, I am not angry
    with You.
Amen.

March 1996

25

Possession

One of my greatest fears is "It."
I cannot touch It, but I can feel It,
And I can sense It with me.
It does not have a smell or taste,
But I can hear It in my trepidating
  spirit.
It has been bothering me
Since my home was broken
Into many times,
And I believe that the root
Of my fears are related
To great fears of a memory.
My fear of It causes me
To touch things again
And again and again
With certain parts of my hands,
Or to check door locks
And light switches again
And again and again.
It seems to control me at times,
But I am working to control It,

By running away, by ignoring It,
By directing my mind to some-
  thing else,
Or sometimes, by standing up to It
Regardless of how plutonic
The situation may be.
Although my mind has been
  threatened
Such that my life revolves around
  my fears,
I am learning to understand
That It can never possess me.
See, in grammar, the word "it"
Can never be possessive;
It can never be contracted into
  ownership.
And so, now that I understand this,
I am trying so hard to believe
That the concept of It
Will never get me, possess me,
  hurt me.
One day, I may finally defeat It.
Then, I can at last live my life
Fearlessly, peacefully, hopefully,
And with gentle happiness.

February 2000

26

About Confidence

Trying new things
Is important.
And, we must believe
In ourselves,
And have confidence
To achieve a goal.
If we don't believe
We can complete a task,
Doubt will take over,
And we may slowly
Back away from the task,
Until we have altogether
Quit working towards the goal.
So, every day,
We must have confidence
In what we are doing.

When we believe in ourselves,
Our spirits become more open
To new things
That are good and healthy.
It also closes up more
To bad and unhealthy
Things in life.
Trying new things
Is important.
And, if we believe
In ourselves,
And have confidence,
We can achieve
So many exciting goals.

May 2000

27

It's Okay, Little Prince

It's okay, Little Prince,
I want to go home, too.
I can see it in your eyes,
I can hear it in your cries,
Can you see it in me, too?
It's okay, Little Prince,
I want to be home, too.
I can sense it in your mind,
I can feel it in your heart-so-kind,
Can you sense it in me, too?
It's okay, Little Prince,
I want to feel home, too.
But for now, I'll help you cope,
And for now, I'll give you hope,
Will you help me out, too?

July 2001

Rolter's Wisdom

You may be tall,
I may be small,
But inside...
We are the same
Length of strength

June 1998

Both Sides

Every privilege
Comes with
A responsibility.
Sounds tough.
Every responsibility
Comes with a privilege.
Sounds durable.

November 2000

33

Thought S'pan

Everyone has a happy thought that
Inspires them to fly into their future...
My happy thought begins with
My mother, who came before me.
My happy thought continues with
My brothers and sister, who are with me.
My happy thought proceeds with
My children, who will come from me.
Everyone has a happy thought that
Inspires them to fly into their future...
My happy thought is kinship.

May 2000

34

Songs of the Wind

Listen to the wind.
If you listen carefully,
You will hear soft notes.
Listen with your mind and
Heart—you will hear a song.
A soft, relaxing song that
Reminds you of peace,
Harmony, and love.
If you hear this song,
Always remember it.
For if you do,
You can teach it
To other people,
And they, too, will forever
Remember their Heartsongs.

July 1998

When the Trees Sing

When the trees sing,
It doesn't really matter
If you know the song,
Or if you know the words,
Or even if you know the tune.
What really matters is knowing
That the trees are singing at all.

May 1998

35

Hope for Life's Journey

Someday,
I'd like to see what's down every road.
I'd like to travel across
Every highway and every byway.
I'd like to explore
Every mountain pass and every sandy trail.
I'd like to follow
Every straight route and every winding path.
Someday,
I'd like to understand
From where all things come,
And to what all things are destined.
Someday,
Even though I am sure of my lesson—
That we are all hoping to the same place—
I'd like to take the time
To travel and explore and follow,
So that I can really see and understand
What's down every road.

August 2001

Hope
for
Our World

About Perseverance

No matter how hard
People strive for peace,
We are not all unified
In the goal, and so,
It is always out of reach
For the world as a whole.
But, it does not, and should not,
Have to be that way.
If we all help each other,
And work together
Day after night after day,
We can achieve a great goal:
World harmony and peace,
For you and me and us.

August 2000

Only One

Only one murder should have been done.
Only one bomb should have been blown.
Oh please, there should have been
Only one hurt to cry out to the Lord.
More than one murder,
More than one bomb,
More than one hurt,
Does not make it right,
Even if saying, "They started the fight!"
Only one of these things was
More than enough.
Only one.
Only one.
But not only one
Can make peace in the world.

February 1998

40

Just Peace

If I could change
One thing in this world,
It would be war.
Instead of war...peace.
But I especially don't want
World War Three,
Because we would
Blow up the earth.
If I could change
One thing in this world
We would have no weapons.
No knives or swords.
No guns or bombs.
Just peace.
Just peace.

February 1998

So What If...

What If the world fills up
With so many people,
That the earth can't hold us all?
Is that a reason for war?
No.
Is that a reason not to love unborn babies?
No.
Is that a reason to let sick people die?
No.
It is a reason we need to make extra room,
First in our hearts, and
Then into our world.
It is a reason to make room for prayer,
Because God is the only "I AM"
Who can answer such a "What If."

February 1998

42

Walking Again

My mother used to walk.
Then, some of her muscles got
  interrupted,
And the vitamins went out,
And she couldn't walk anymore.
This is a poem about her walking
  again.
I remember her throwing me up in
  the air.
I felt myself flying, going way up
  high.
But now, she can't give me that
  gift.
So, I made her a card, a gift,
With a picture of her walking again,
And throwing me up in the air.
I love my mother.
I wish she was walking again.
All the other parts of this story,
All the beginning before here in
  the poem,
Well, that was the prologue.
Now, this is my story, about
  walking again.
My mommy used to walk—I
  remember it.
I really miss Jamie and Katie and
  Stevie,
But I also miss her walking.

I wish she could be walking again.
She could be swinging me around,
To and fro, up and down, in the
  beanbag.
She could be playing tag with me.
She could be out on the swings.
She could be walking again,
Up the stairs, or all around.
I really miss her walking.
I wish that we could find a medicine
That would make her muscles
  get stronger.
Some other people could only
  crawl on earth
But now they can walk again up in
  Heaven.
I can still walk,
But I wish the two of us could be
Walking again, together.
I wish that we could be a walking
  family.
I really love my mom, even
  though she can't walk.
I love God, and He loves us,
Even the people who can't walk.
I love my mommy and it's okay,
Even if this is the end of walking
  again.

July 1996

30

Been There

Mommy,
You're in
A bad mood,
Aren't you?
You're sad, and
You're angry,
Aren't you?
You're being
A little bit nasty,
Aren't you?
I bet that
You're missing Jamie
A lot right now,
Aren't you?
That's okay, Mommy.
I get sad
And angry
And a little bit nasty, too,
When I am missing Jamie.
Do you need
To be held and rocked?
Here,
I'll give you a
Hug and a kiss.

June 1994

About Dreamland

There is a place called Dreamland.
It is where you travel about
When you first rest into sleep.
You dream that you are in clouds
With ladders and stairs that lead you
Until you get to Dreamland's castle.
In the castle, there are pictures,
Lots of pictures,
And the pictures are good dreams.
Watch your step, though,
Or you might get sucked into the ground.
And in the ground are bad dreams.
In the good dream pictures,
You still watch your steps carefully,
Because the dreams are all the ones
Of your life, and also some more.
They are all of what was or almost was,
And what might be even if it's good or bad.
You can choose any one of the pictures
That you want, so relax and take your time.
Look around and you will see that
There are millions and millions and
More people there, finding dreams and
Jumping into the pictures to their thoughts.
And now, I will leave you tonight, and everynight,
In the Kingdom of Dreamland.
Jump into the good dreams,
But step carefully watching for the bad dreams.
Sleep well, and good night.

September 1997

32

Salvation

The world must
Never waste
A memory,
No matter
How it
Makes one feel.
For every
Memory is a
Gift of God.
And, every
Gift of God
That the world uses
Is another step
Towards
Each-otherness,
And peace.

June 2000

In a Mountain Storm Cloud

We were up in
The mountains,
High in the sky.
It was raining.
But we were not
As wet.
For we were in the
Mountain storm cloud,
Understanding the rain
As it went down, down
Below the valley.
We were up in
The Heavens,
Watering the earth below,
Washing away the sadness
That grows from
Anger and fear.

August 1998

44

The Bigger Picture

Mommy said we should pray
For the little children
And the grown-ups who died
When the mean and nasty
Men put a bomb in the building
In Oklahoma.
I will pray for them,
But they are all in Heaven.
We are sad,
But they are happy.
I think who we really
Need to pray for
Are the men who
Did such a sad thing.
They are the ones who
Do not have God in their hearts.
They are the ones who
Will not go to Heaven
When they die.
So I think we should
Pray for them, too,
So that maybe
They will learn to be sorry
For what they did,
And learn to be good people.

April 1995

45

When Warnings Are Ignored

Right now,
The whole world is "Mr. Yuk."
The little children know to stay away
When they see the stickers and
  the signs.
The big people don't see them though,
But that's because they close
Their own eyes...you know.
They don't want to see the
Warnings and poisons of war.
How it kills our children,
Our people, our earth.
They have "reasons" for fighting
Anyplace, Anywhere.
They have "reasons" for killing in
Bosnia, Iraq, and Zaire.
They fight about God
And how people pray.
They fight about fighting...

They just fight and fight
And fight, Everyday.
There is anger in families
And even in schools.
People don't want to follow
The laws and the rules...
Unless they made them or like them.
But that is not right.
That just isn't right.
That thinking just poisons
Respect and responsibility
  and life.
Poisoned thoughts
Turn into poisoned actions,
Which causes the war and fight.
And so,
Even though we should see
The warning signs Everywhere,
We don't look with our hearts,
And the whole world is "Mr. Yuk."

March 1998

46

Past, Present, Future

Shrouded in white,
Dark ninja knight.
Hooded, each man,
Dreadful east Klan.
Masked to be super,
Wicked storm trooper.
Marching in rows,
Planning low blows.
No soul to claim,
Unspeakable name.
Evil of hatin'…
Army of Satan.

February 2001

Attack on America

A wild bomb will consume
Morning, evening, and all people,
Showering dirt to burn man's skin.

September 11, 2001

47

9-11...2001

It was a dark day in America.
There was no amazing grace.
Freedom did not ring.
Tragedy attacked sky-high.
Fiery terror reigned.
Structures collapsed.
Red with blood, white with ash,
And out-of-the-sky blue.
As children trust elders,
Citizens find faith in leaders.
But all were blinded,
Shocked by the blasts.
Undefiable outrage.
Undeniable outpouring
Of support, even prayer,
Or at least, moments of silence.
Church and State
Could not be separated.
A horrific blasting of events
With too few happy endings.
Can the children sleep
Safely in their beds tonight?
Can the citizens ever rest
Assured of national security again?
God, please, bless America...
And the rest of our earthly home.

September 11, 2001

48

For Our World

We need to stop.
Just stop.
Stop for a moment...
Before anybody
Says or does anything
That may hurt anyone else.
We need to be silent.
Just silent.
Silent for a moment...
Before we forever lose
The blessing of songs
That grow in our hearts.
We need to notice.
Just notice.
Notice for a moment...
Before the future slips away
Into ashes and dust of humility.

Stop, be silent, and notice...
In so many ways, we are the same.
Our differences are unique treasures.
We have, we are, a mosaic of gifts
To nurture, to offer, to accept.
We need to be.
Just be.
Be for a moment...
Kind and gentle, innocent and
   trusting,
Like children and lambs,
Never judging or vengeful
Like the judging and vengeful.
And now, let us pray,
Differently, yet together,
Before there is no earth, no life,
No chance for peace.

September 2001

49

Peace

The sun feels warm on our bodies and hands.
But, if we touch the sun, it would burn.
It makes things bright and beautiful,
But, if we look at it, it hurts our eyes.
The sun doesn't make any noise,
And we can't taste it, or smell it.
I guess that's why the sun stays
So far away from us.
The sun is our friend,
But we can't do anything with it,
And we can't touch it or look at it,
Except when it first comes in the morning,
Or when it is leaving in the evening.
Then we can look at the
Sunrise and the sunset,
And see how wonderful
Our friend the sun is.
But we still can't touch it,
Because it would hurt, and
Friends don't hurt friends.

October 1993

Morning Gift

Don't you love the mornings
When you go outside,
And there on the ground
Is a fresh, perfect, green leaf?
A leaf, floated from the
Quiet summer trees,
Just resting on the grass, and
Waiting to be discovered.
Touch the treasure, and
Pick it up gently, then
Feel all the excitement of
A new leaf, with no tears,
No marks, no holes.
It is a sign of healing and future.
Don't you just love the mornings
When you are reminded of
The special gifts of life?

June 1999

52

Revolutions 365.25

When the moon sets
Over your shoulder
As the sun rises
Bright towards your face,
What's in the middle?
Your life is...
Filled with choices
For each moment, each place.
We live between the
Past and the future,
In the moment of our
Here, now, today.
Can we cope with the
Daily life stresses?
If we humbly accept...
We must pray.

December 2001

53

Life Is Like...

Life is like a story book...
Although we aren't
Able to talk with
Dragons and fly far into space,
Each day is like
A new chapter,
With new lessons
For our lives.
Life is like a dream...
Although we don't
Know what kind of
Reverie we will have,
Each day is like
A new thought,
With new hopes
For our lives.
Life is like a great waiting...
Although we can't
Realize when or how,
Each day is like
A new chance,
With new opportunities
For our lives.

As we travel and learn
And think and hope
And chance opportunities
In each day of our lives,
We must understand
That anytime
Could be the Time
That we face the fact of Heaven,
And never have to fear again.
So each day,
We should live out
The great dream and story
That our lives are waiting to be...
For we know
And we are able
And we realize that
Life is like
Whatever we create it to be.

August 2000

54

Future Reminiscing

It is good
To have a past
That is pleasant
To reflect upon.
Take care
To create
Such a gift
For your future.

December 2000

The Way Home

Sometimes the way home is love.
Sometimes the way home is together.
And sometimes the way home is
Not just love,
But loving each other.
And sometimes the way home is
Not just together,
But together with other people...
  People you love a lot,
  People you like a lot, and
  People you are friends with.
But all of the times, the way home is
Every good thing that God told us to do.

January 1996

56

Momentous Reality

The next century, the next millennium
Is being made, now, Today, each
  second.
We could be working towards
World peace, living as one spirit.
Or, we could be working towards
Disaster, chemical and nuclear
  wars.
The harmony, and existence of
  the future
Depends on the harmony and
  existence
Of each individual here, today.
We must be brave going into the
  future.
We must remember to play after
  each storm.
We must not live in fear of bad
  things
Blocking our way or overcoming
  our optimism.
If we can work together to face
  the future,
If we can unite as one,
Then our future will look, and be,
  very bright.

Even though the future seems far
  away,
It is actually beginning right now.
And while we are living in the
  present,
We must celebrate life everyday,
Knowing that we are becoming
  history
With every word, every action, every
  moment.
Because we, today, are the history
  of tomorrow,
We must ask ourselves each day
What we are doing that may have
An influence on the future.
It really won't be for many years that
The future will indicate if something
  we said,
Or if something we did or did not do,
Had an impact on a single individual,
Or if it trickled out to touch the
  whole world.

February 2000

57

Faith Imagery

I can imagine non-existence.
Can you?
It's not like being dead,
But it's not being alive.
There is no light,
But the dark is nothingness.
It is not painful,
But it feels horrible.
It is being stuck
Between not having been,
And having been but being gone.
There is no feeling in non-existence,
But it is the most alone thing
Of loneliness one could imagine.
I can imagine non-existence.
I thank God everyday,
For the gift of faith...
For it is in faith,
That I will exist, forever.
I can imagine non-existence,
And I hope and pray
That you can, too,
For Ever.

October 1999

Believing in Someday

Maybe,
Someday,
We will all join hands
And live together...
Helping each other,
Loving each other.
Maybe,
Someday,
We will all make the world
A much better place...
And be like a gigantic,
Smoothly rushing river of peace—
A loving circle that nothing can break.
Maybe,
Someday,
We may start with just one person,
And one permanent peace agreement
Within one's self, within one's world.

Personal peace can then spread
Within and between the families,
Then within and between communities,
And then within and around the
   whole world.
Maybe,
Someday,
We can become
As close to perfect
As anything and anyone can get.
Let us each join our own Heartsong
With this old song of the heart, and
   believe...
   "Let there be peace on earth,
   And let it begin with me."

August 2000

59

Facing the Future

Every journey begins
With but a small step.
And every day is a chance
For a new, small step
In the right direction.
Just follow your Heartsong.

December 1998

Index

Journey
Through
Heartsongs

Journey
Through
Heartsongs

Written and Illustrated by
Mattie J.T. Stepanek
Poet and Peacemaker

VSP Books
HYPERION
New York

ISBN: 0-7868-6942-9

Hyperion books are available for special promotions and premiums.
For details contact Hyperion Special Markets, 77 West 66th Street,
11th floor, New York, New York, 10023, or call 212-456-0100.

FIRST EDITION

10 9 8 7

Dedication

This book is dedicated to Katie, Stevie and Jamie,
and to all the other angels, saints and blessed ones
who guide, guard and protect me, especially
Jude Thaddeus, Rita and Andre Bisset.

—Love, Mattie

Dear Friends,

Mattie and his mother, Jeni, are two of the most extraordinary people we have been privileged to meet. As this book shows, Mattie, poet and peacemaker, is a gifted writer with a powerful message for those seeking hope, faith and answers. We thank God for blessing us with the opportunity to publish Mattie's books and to help spread his messages of hope, peace, wisdom and insight to people everywhere.

But we could not have done it alone. We wish to acknowledge the following people for their help and support in producing this book: our mom, Shirley Shaw, for showing up at the office every day and leading the charge with joy and enthusiasm; our dad, Chuck Shaw, for keeping us organized and well fed during this busy time; Martha Shaw Whitley, our amazing sister for all of her hard work; Marissa L. Garis of the Children's National Medical Center in Washington, DC, for introducing us to Mattie and Jeni; our webmaster, David Schaefer, for keeping our website constantly up-to-date; and Catherine Morrison in our office, for keeping the production line going. We also want to thank: Jeff Biggs; George Muriithi; Moshe Koenick; Ron Cofone; Lisa Delnegro; Kim Turpin Davis; Rep. Fred Upton (R-MI); Ron Landsman, attorney-at-law; Tim O'Brien, attorney-at-law; Sharon Taylor; and the Encouragers Class at First Baptist Church of Alexandria, VA, which planted the seed.

And, most of all, Mattie and Jeni.

Peter and Cheryl Barnes
Publishers

September 2001

Acknowledgments

I would like to thank Dr. Robert Fink, Dr. Christie Corrveaux, Dr. Kim Fenton, and everybody at the Pediatric Intensive Care Unit at Children's National Medical Center in Washington, DC, for believing in my life and my future.

I would like to thank Peter and Cheryl Barnes, Shirley Shaw, Martha Whitley, Marissa Garis, and Maggie and Kate Jerde for believing in my dreams.

I would like to thank the Muscular Dystrophy Association, Jerry Lewis, Children's Hospice International, Harold Schaitberger and the International Association of Fire Fighters, the Harley-Davidson Owners Group, the D'Anna "MARS" Family, United Airlines and many others for believing in hope towards a cure.

I would like to thank Jimmy Carter, my "humble peacemaker" hero, and Oprah Winfrey, Ed McMahon, Rosie O'Donnell, Martin Doblmeier, Jeanne Myers and Steven Spielberg for believing in and fulfilling the wishes of children.

I would like to thank Sandy, Heather, Jamie-D., Chris, Lyn, Mike, Nick, Ben, Shana, Bubby, Flora, Paul, Don, Lorraine, Clifton, Valerie, Mollie, Katie, Annie, Ron, Devin, Gina, Ann, Casey, Jim, Andi, Leslie, Bert, J.J., Randy, Roger, Holy Rosary and many other kin-family for believing in and supporting the journey through Heartsongs.

And, I would like to thank my mom, Jeni, for believing in all of these things and in the daily celebration of life and spirit. I love you and you love me, forever and always.

—Love
Mattie J. T. Stepanek

Foreword

Mattie Stepanek is my personal friend and one of the most remarkable young people I have ever known. He wants to be a peacemaker; and through his poems and own courageous example, he proves that finding peace within one's self can lead to harmony among families, communities and nations. With wisdom and uncomplicated vision Mattie reminds us how easy it is to forgive others, to find something amazing even in the most trivial things and to celebrate the little gifts of life each day.

Journey Through Heartsongs will inspire readers of all ages with thoughts and images that bring both tears and expanded hearts.

—Jimmy Carter
Former U.S. President

CONTENTS

Prayer for a Journey

Thank You, God,
Not just for life,
But for our journey through life.
Life is a miracle,
And a journey through life
Is so full of so many more miracles
If we travel with our Heartsongs.
Thank You, God,
For blessing me with the
Gift of Heartsongs,
So that I can enjoy my miracles.

April 1998

About the Author

I am Mattie J.T. Stepanek.
My body has light skin,
Red blood, blue eyes, and blond hair.
Since I have mitochondrial myopathy,
I even have a trach, a ventilator, and oxygen.
Very poetic, I am, and very smart, too.
I am always brainstorming ideas and stories.
I am a survivor, but some day, I will see
My two brothers and one sister in Heaven.
When I grow up, I plan to become
A father, a writer, a public speaker,
And most of all, a peacemaker.
Whoever I am, and whatever happens,
I will always love my body and mind,
Even if it has different abilities
Than other peoples' bodies and minds.
I will always be happy, because
I will always be me.

May 2001

Heartsong

I have a song, deep in my heart,
And only I can hear it.
If I close my eyes and sit very still
It is so easy to listen to my song.
When my eyes are open and
I am so busy and moving and busy,
If I take time and listen very hard,
I can still hear my Heartsong.
It makes me feel happy.
Happier than ever.
Happier than everywhere
And everything and everyone
In the whole wide world.
Happy like thinking about
Going to Heaven when I die.
My Heartsong sounds like this—
> *I love you! I love you!*
> *How happy you can be!*
> *How happy you can make*
> *This whole world be!*

And sometimes it's other
Tunes and words, too,
But it always sings the
Same special feeling to me.
It makes me think of
Jamie, and Katie and Stevie,
And other wonderful things.
This is *my* special song.
But do you know what?
All people have a special song
Inside their hearts!
Everyone in the whole wide world
Has a special Heartsong.
If you believe in magical, musical hearts,
And if you believe you can be happy,
Then you, too, will hear *your* song.

March 1996

Crystal Celebration

Sometimes,
Sunrise is like a heavenly crystal ball.
Everyday,
In the little bit of time between night and day,
The Angels look at the earth
To see how things have been and
To see how things are going and
To see how things will be.
The sky changes from dark
Into Angel-whites and Angel-golds.
The blackness of trees starts to glow with
Pinks and purples and oranges from their hearts.
And during each dawn,
All the Angels gather up and have
A celebration in God's honor!
And sometimes,
You can even watch
And join them in the celebrating.
Just look out into the sunrise,
Then jump into your own heart,
Float into the air like in a dream,
And pray with love and praise and thank-yous
For your life, for your spirit, for your sunrise...
And for being a part of this heavenly crystal ball!

December 1996

For Mr. Thompson

The people who like poetry are special.
They are the same people who hear
Lullabies and wind chimes
When the birds are noisy together.
They are the ones who see
Star-gifts in every season —
Tree-stars in the fall,
Snow-stars in the winter,
Dandelion-fairy-stars in the spring, and
Lightning-bug-stars in the summer.
They are the ones who have
Favorite colors that are wonderful gifts
Like sunset or rainbow or treasure.
They are the ones who have a
Song in their heart and
Words in their mind that
Come together and slip out
Into the air or onto paper as a gift
To someone else, or even themselves.
The people who like poetry are probably
The ones who really like life,
And who know how to celebrate
Even when things are sad or happy.
We remember that sometimes,
Even if we don't understand why,
That the rain falls for a reason.
We remember how important it is
To play after a storm, just because
We need to keep playing and living.
And, we are the people who remember
To say thank You to God for our gifts.

May 1996

Touch of Heaven

What is it like to have a baby
Fall asleep while holding your finger?
It is a soft, precious touch.
It is relaxing, yet exciting.
It is a feeling of trust and importance.
It is so soothing it makes me want to
Fall asleep.
It is a sign of peace and love.
What is it like to have a baby
Fall asleep while holding your finger?
It is a great gift from Heaven.

November 1999

The Language of God

Do you know what
Language God speaks?
God speaks Every-Language.
That's because God made
Everyone and gave
Everyone different languages.
And God understands all of them.
And, do you know what is God's
Favorite language?
God's favorite language is
Not grown-up's language,
But the Language of Children.
That's because children
Are special to God.
Children know how to share,
And they never lose
Their Heartsongs.

April 1996

A Handful of Mattie

My fingers stand for
Reader,
Writer,
Black Belt,
Collector,
And friend...
My palm stands for
Heartsongs,
Ebullient, spiritual,
Honest, trustworthy,
Brother, uniparental,
Optimistic, inspiring,
Diligent, savant,
Peacemaker, and
"Gift of God" —
My hands raise in prayer for
Giving thanks for my being
Which stands for life.

January 2000

Reader

Writer, poet

Black Belt

Collector

Friend

Heartsongs
Ebullient, Spirited
Honest, Trustworthy
Brother, Uniparental
Optimistic, Inspiring
Diligent, Savant
Peacemaker
"Gift of
God"

9

Making Real Sense of the Senses

Our eyes are for looking at things,
But they are also for crying
When we are very happy or very sad.
Our ears are for listening,
But so are our hearts.
Our noses are for smelling food,
But also the wind and the grass and
If we try very hard, butterflies.
Our hands are for feeling,
But also for hugging and touching so gently.
Our mouths and tongues are for tasting,
But also for saying words, like
"I love you," and
"Thank You, God, for all of these things."

April 1995

Climbing to Heaven

In the winter, trees reach
Up to touch the sky.
Without their leaves,
The trees look like hands
And fingers stretching up
So, so, so high.
And if you look at the
Tallest tree in our backyard,
You can see that it is
So, so, so close to Heaven.
Perhaps we could go out
And climb
Up the tree,
Up the hand,
Up the fingers,
And into the sky.
Then, we could just step
Through the clouds,
... And into Heaven.

January 1996

About Angels

Do you know what Angels wear?
They wear
Angel-halos and Angel-wings, and
Angel-dresses and Angel-shirts under them, and
Angel-underwear and Angel-shoes and Angel-socks, and
On their heads
They wear
Angel-hair —
Except if they don't have any hair.
Some children and grown-ups
Don't have any hair because they
Have to take medicine that makes it fall out.
And sometimes,
The medicine makes them all better.
And sometimes,
The medicine doesn't make them all better,
And they die.
And they don't have any Angel-hair.
So do you know what God does then?
He gives them an
Angel-wig.
And that's what Angels wear.

January 1995

Believing for the Journey

Every day,
Everyone in the world
Should do at least
One thing nice for others.
Doing so can help each person
Believe in himself or herself
More fully, and
Give confidence that may
Inspire each person
To do more and
More new and good things
For the self,
For others, and
For the world.
Those positive attitudes
And actions
Can be the first of many steps
Towards the journey
For world peace.
And world peace,
Harmony, and
Confidence are essential
For our future.

May 2000

Future Echo

When I swing,
I go everywhere,
And yet,
Nowhere at all.
It's like being
In the middle
Of an echo,
That hasn't left me yet,
And so,
It hasn't come back.
I am between
Yesterday and tomorrow,
But still in my life of now.
When I swing,
I feel so happy,
And excited, and peaceful,

And yet,
I feel a little bit lonely
About the time that
Will come, when I will not be
Able to swing, anymore.
And so, for now,
When I swing,
I move back and forth
In the everywhere
And the nowhere
That is the understanding
Of an echo —
The echo of my spirit
That grows from my life,
And that sounds like
A peaceful, but lonely cry,
For the times
When I swing
Before I die.

August 1999

Vietnam War Memorial

A wall gives structure.
It can divide and block.
It can support and fortify.
It can be a place to display
Photos, writings, awards,
And memories.
But this, is The Wall.
The Wall that gives structure
To the insane losses of a war.
The Wall that represents
A nation divided and blocked.
The Wall that supports too
Many broken hearts and bodies.
The Wall that fortifies the reality
Of dead lives among the living.
The Wall that reflects memories
Of what was, of what is,
Of what might have been,

16

In photos, in letters and poems,
In medals of honor and dedication,
And in teddy bears, and flowers,
And tears and tears and tears.
This is The Wall,
Born out of pain and anguish
And guilt,
That gives names to the children
Of grieving mothers and fathers
And to the spouses of widows
And to parents of wondering children.
This is The Wall
That echoes sadness and fear,
Yet whispers relief and hope.
This is The Wall.
May we be forever blessed by its
Structure and fortitude and support,
And may we be forever reminded
Of the eternal divisions of war.

February 2000

The Tiger Fights a
Dragon in the Purple Sun

When the sun sets,
In the mist,
The tiger and
The dragon fight
In the purple light.
Who wins?
Who knows?
Thy who have
Great Heartsongs know.
The tiger of peace, or
The dragon of anger.

May 1998

Philosophy Glass

Some people see a glass
With some water in it and say,
"Oh yes, that glass is half full!"
Some people see a glass
With some water in it and say,
"Oh no, that glass is half empty!"
I hope that I am one of the
People who is always able to
Look at each of my glasses and
See them as at least half full.
That's very important in life,
Because if you live feeling like
Your glass is half empty, well,
It may as well be empty all the way.

May 1997

On Being a Champion

A champion is a winner,
A hero...
Someone who never gives up
Even when the going gets rough.
A champion is a member of
A winning team...
Someone who overcomes challenges
Even when it requires creative solutions.
A champion is an optimist,
A hopeful spirit...
Someone who plays the game,
Even when the game is called life...
Especially when the game is called life.
There can be a champion in each of us,
If we live as a winner,
If we live as a member of the team,
If we live with a hopeful spirit,
For life.

September 1999

Peace of Patience

I cannot wait to become
A peacemaker.
I cannot wait to help
The world overcome
Anger, and problems of evil.
I cannot wait for the world
To be peaceful,
And for everyone
To live in harmony.
I cannot wait to grow
And be and overcome.
But, I will wait,
With patience,
And hope, and peace.

November 1999

Faces of Faith

I wish that the people who have
Anger and hatred and sadness
Will remember about their Heartsongs,
And get them back.
Everyone is born with a Heartsong,
But as we grow up,
Sometimes we forget about it,
Because we don't listen to it enough.
And the people of war, well,
They really need to get them back.
Their Heartsongs really need to live,
Because when we die,
They are what rise up.
I want that to happen to me.
I want my Heartsong to rise up, and
I am trying my best down here on earth.
You really can go to Heaven.
Everyone can.
But sometimes,
You have to sit in ThinkTime
When you lose your Heartsong.

And that is sad because some people
Who go sit in ThinkTime,
They never come back.
And some people just think and realize,
And then they come back.
But if we remember to listen to our Heartsongs,
We will not need to go to ThinkTime.
Our songs will just rise up out of our hearts,
And take our spirits straight on to Heaven.
I will remember to listen to my Heartsong.
I will remind others, especially the grown-ups,
To listen to their Heartsongs, too.
And for the people who have forgotten theirs,
I will share mine with them.
Maybe they will keep mine, and
Maybe it will remind them of their own.
But what really matters is that we
Keep the faces of faith, and
Listen to our Heartsongs, and live
So that we can die and Live again.

July 1996

Welkin

The sky is such
A perfect blue,
It must have
Been painted there.
Even the clouds
Bear witness
To the stroke of
An artist's brush.
This just proves that
God is perfect
At many professions.

February 2000

Pirate-Candy

You know why most people
Don't like black jelly-beans?
Because they're pirate-candy!
Black jelly-beans taste like "pirate."
They smell like pirate.
They're the color of the
Jolly Roger pirate flag.
They're like the little black patch
Pirates wear over their empty-eye.
Black jelly-beans are also the
Pirates' favorite candy flavor,
Because they taste a little bit mean.
But under the hard black-bean outside,
Is a soft good-jelly inside
That tastes sweet and nice.
You see,
Most people just taste the dark part.
But I crunch through that nasty bit
And get right to the jelly-bean guts.
So I am the lucky one,
Because I know that most pirate-candy
Is actually pretty good stuff.

April 1996

Important Things

When I grow up,
I think maybe
I will be a snowman,
Because when it
Snows outside,
I'll already be cold
And like it.
And children will
Play with me,
And laugh
And sing
And dance
All around me.
And those are important
Things to have happen
When you grow up.

December 1993

26

Beware, of The Ever-Wolf

I am a werewolf for any moon...
When the moon sits full like a
Yellow-white or maybe orange circle
In the dark night sky,
I will grow my fur, and
My long pointy fingernails, and
My longer pointy toenails, and
My two fuzzy tails, and
My icky-sharp'ed fangs, and...
I will howl,
Ow, ow, ow, ow-oooooooohhhh!!!!
Under the full moon.
Then, I will come back inside,
And turn back into the
Nice little here-boy that I am...
Except that,
I am a werewolf for any moon.
So even if I don't have my fur
And my nails and my teeth
And my lonely, scary howl,
I will be there just the same.
I will be a whenwolf with the sun, and
A whichwolf with the almost moons, and
A whywolf with the invisible moon.
But always watch out, and beware, because
I am a werewolf for any moon...

May 1996

At Long Last

Half-empty trees
Scritch at
Ghouly gray skies,
Laughing black crow
Haunts a sound
To the wise,
Orange-toothed
Pumpkins smirk
Jagged tooth grins,
Message is clear:
Halloween now begins!

October 1998

The Left-Over Child

A long time ago, my parents
Had a little girl named Katie.
They thought that they would only
Have this one little child,
But then mommy started growing
Another little baby inside of her.
It was a little boy named Stevie.
But little Katie died, and
Then little Stevie died, and
My parents were alone
Without any children at all.
Then, they grew another baby.
It was a little boy named Jamie.
And then in 1990, they had
Another little boy named Mattie,
And Jamie and Mattie were
Brothers together for a long time.
But then, Jamie died, too,
But Mattie was still alive because
He didn't die like his brothers and sister.
Now, he's not really a little brother anymore,
But he's not really the only child either.
Mattie is the left-over child,
All alone with the parents of dead children.

February 1996

Unanswered Questions

My brother, Jamie died.
His muscles-and-bones
Did not work at all anymore.
His happiness and specialness
Went into Heaven and
His body got buried in
The hole that goes into the ground
And then into the sky and
And then to the Everywhere
And Forever that is Heaven.
I know why he died,
But I also don't know why.
I really don't.
He is happy,
And sometimes I am, too.
And sometimes I am sad
Or angry or scared or confused.
And sometimes I think
That maybe,
I didn't hold his hand tight enough.

December 1993

Anniversary Reflections

I remember the day Jamie died.
Except...
I didn't know that Jamie DIED
Because I didn't know
What it was like to look or be dead.
I remember you told me Jamie died, and
I remember that his tubing wasn't on his trach, and
I remember that you wouldn't let me
Get in bed with Jamie that morning.
But I thought it was because Jamie was asleep.
I thought when I got home from school that
You would let me get in bed and play and read
And be with my brother Jamie.
But when I got home, Jamie was still asleep,
Except...
He was really dead.
I remember that, but I didn't know that.
I remember all the people coming over
And going into Jamie's room, but
His music was playing, and
His nurses were there, and
He looked just the same in his bed,
So I never really knew he was dead.
I remember the day we went to church
And then to the cemetery to bury Jamie's body.
Except...
I didn't know that I wouldn't see him again.
I remember you put him in that little white box,
And you showed me how comfortable his body looked,

And I put a picture of us in his hand
With his cross and his Mr. Bear and his Blue-Bunny-Rabbit,
And I knew that we should Never put Jamie in a box on the floor
But it must be okay because
The nurses were helping you.
I remember the little white box in church and
I remember thinking that it was time for Jamie
To knock on the box and we would open it and
He would sit up and yell, "BOO!" and we would all laugh.
I remember that you said this was
A celebration for Jamie at church,
So I knew it was just a game and that he would come out.
Except...
He didn't.
And the box got all buried into Heaven but under the ground,
With Jamie inside of it, because
He was dead.
I remember the day Jamie died,
And I understand now that it means Forever
And that he wasn't asleep and couldn't yell "BOO."
But I don't understand why you sent me to school that day.
If you knew that dead was Forever,
Why did you send me to school?
I should have stayed home like you,
To be with Jamie before he went
Forever into his little white box,
Because I want to remember Jamie,
Forever.

November 1995

Never-ending Story

Once upon a time,
There was a Jamie and a Mattie.
And for a while,
They were both alive.
But one day,
Jamie died.
And of that,
Mattie cried.
And this story goes
On and on and on
With a Jamie dying
And a Mattie crying,
And on and on like that
Ever- and After-after.

August 1994

Before the Visit

The rising sun sends
Wisps of light through
Streaking clouds,
But the blackbirds play under
The empty willow tree.
The midnight of the fall
Is rising upon us,
And against us.
It is the dawn of winter.
There are things
In the clouds, and
We must be prepared.
We must be watchful,
As the blackbirds,
As the weeping willow,
As the waiting darkness.

December 1997

Intensive Sense

In the PICU...
I see bright lights,
But there is no sun,
And almost a loss of time.
I hear machines alarming,
But though they ring warnings,
Lives are not always saved.
I feel pain, intense at moments.
But I also feel the hurt of anxiety,
And neither anguish is good for the spirit.
Someday,
I will leave the PICU, again.
I will see the sun,
Rising into new days,
But I will know it must set, too soon.
I will hear music sounding,
Ringing from so many instruments,
But most of it will be memories of my Heartsongs.
I will feel my spirit rejuvenated,
And I will be filled with hope again.
But, I will feel a sad sense of loss
For the children
Who will be Still
With the anguished sounding loss of time...
In the PICU.

May 2001

PICU—Pediatric Intensive Care Unit

Rebecca's Reminder

It is sad
When a friend
Dies.
Death becomes
Suddenly
Painful.
Suddenly
Real.
Suddenly
Reminding.
When a friend
Dies,
Perhaps
We should
Suddenly
Remember
How real
Death is,
And wonder
How our
LIFE
Will be,
Suddenly,
Based on
How much of
A friend we are
Now,
Regularly.

November 2000

The Holding-On Family

I'll never let you go, Mommy.
And you never let me go, either.
We'll hold on to each other,
Forever.
We'll never let go.
Even if you get very, very sick,
Or if I get very, very sick,
We'll never let go.
We'll hold on, and
We'll pray for each other,
Together.
Our family already got enough smaller
Without Jamie, and Katie and Stevie.
We need to never let go again.
We'll be a whole family,
Staying together, you and me.
We'll be a holy family,
Praying, together.
We'll be a holding-on family,
Forever.

April 1996

About Wishing

Some people think that
Wishing is childish.
But, wishing is
For everybody.
Wishing can help the
Old feel young, and
Wishing can help the
Young grow into the
Wisdom of age.
Wishing is not
Prayer or magic,
But, somewhere in between.
Like prayer and magic,
Wishing brings optimism,
And wishing brings hope.
And like prayer and magic,
Wishing brings new ideas,
And sometimes,
The touch of new life.
And that, is essential
For our future.

January 2000

Heavenly Greeting

Dear God,
For a long time,
I have wondered about
How You will meet me
When I die and come to
Live with You in Heaven.
I know You reach out
Your hand to welcome
Your people into Your home,
But I never knew if You
Reached out Your right hand,
Or if You
Reached out Your left hand.
But now I don't have to
Wonder about that anymore.
I asked my mommy and
She told me that You
Reach out both of Your hands,
And welcome us with
A great big giant hug.
Wow!
I can't wait for my hug, God.
Thank You,
And Amen.

March 1996

On Growing Up (Part V)
We are growing up.
We are many colors of skin.
We are many languages.
We are many ages and sizes.
We are many countries...
But we are one earth.
We each have one heart.
We each have one life.
We are growing up, together,
So we must each join our
Hearts and lives together
And live as one family.

September 1996

On Growing Up (Part I)

I really don't know much
About my toilet.
I need to learn more about it,
And about how it works.
I need to learn all
About my house
Before I grow up,
So I can teach my kids
Before they grow up,
So they can teach their kids
Before they grow up,
And you see, it can just go
On and on and on like that.
There's a lot of learning to do
While we are growing up,
And a lot of teaching
And a lot of learning
While we are all grown up.

January 1996

Be a Bird

Birds walk in the sky.
I wonder
What it would be like to
Walk in the sky.
I will be a bird,
And walk in the sky.
The air is
Very, very cold way up high.
And the sun is
Like a bumblebee,
All yellow and round.
And the dark rain clouds are
Like lots and lots of bumblebees,
All angry and buzzing and angry.
The sky is so blue, and
The butterflies are so orange, and
The ground is
So way down below.

October 1993

Sunset

Beautiful things
Are everywhere,
But sunset is so
Soothing and peaceful.
It can send you
Into Dreamland,
Filled with happy thoughts.
And it's all just because
The sunset is God's
Special Tiger's Eye.
A Tiger's Eye is
Sometimes dark and stormy,
Sometimes bright with colors.
A Tiger's Eye is strong
And seeing and knowing,
And it is always a
Symbol of life end energy.
So when you see the sunset,
Through storms and brights,
Think of God,
Our great I AM,
And His beautiful Tiger's Eye.

February 1998

Hidden Treasure

After-the-storm clouds
Are like pirate treasure chests...
Dark and gray-black and
Sometimes a little scary looking.
But just look behind as they open...
Silver and shiny-gold and
Usually bright and warm, if it's
Still daytime after the storm.

May 1996

Grounded Lesson

Life is a treasure.
People should enjoy it,
Even if digging
To it, or
Through it,
Is a challenge.

February 2000

Tree Song

The trees are singing tonight.
Listen... listen and hear...
They're singing a song of happiness and joy.
They're singing a song of peace and thought.
They're singing a song of wonder and God.
I do not know the name of the song,
But I know the sound of the music.
I do not know the words of the song,
But I know the feel of the sound.
And the sounds make me feel brave and proud.
I feel relaxed and trusting as a lamb.
I am ready to run and play.
I am ready to rest gently.
I am ready to comfort someone.
And, I am ready to follow my Shepherd
To a good life, which is Heaven.
The trees are singing tonight.
Listen... listen and hear...

May 1998

46

Christmas Stars

In December,
The dark sky of nighttime
Comes very early.
And as soon as the daytime
And then the sunset are all through,
There are lots and lots of
Christmas stars.
We see them everywhere
In the sky with the moon.
It is a present from
Heaven in the sky
To real live people
Who look up.
That is so special.

December 1993

About Watches

I like wearing
Lots of watches
For two reasons.
First,
If they are all set
A little different,
No one's ever
Too late, or
Too early, or
Right on time.
They just "are."
Second,
With all these
Watches on me,
It's like having
"All the time
In the world!"
And never having
To think about
The end of time,
Or about dying.

August 1997

Swinging

So high...
Wind tickles my tummy
Plays with my feet
Gives my hair a ride.
So high...
Grab a leaf from a tree
Reach a so-far-up branch
See over the edge of my earth.
So high...
Meditate on being
Touch all my thoughts
Think about friends
And families and
Brothers and sisters.
So high...
Leave this world for a bit
Jump into Heaven for a moment
Then, swing back into my life again.
So high...

August 1998

Kindergarten-itis

My stuffed animals and babies
Don't like the big yellow monster.
They don't like that big yellow monster
That swallows Mattie up every morning,
And then takes him away for so many hours
And then brings him back home
And then spits him out "p-tooey"
Right where it ate him in the first place.
Even when Mattie tells them,
"It's only a school bus little guys,
I can handle it, don't you worry!"
They still don't like it at all.
But now, there are only
Seventeen days left for that
Big yellow monster to swallow me
And chew me and spit me out "p-tooey…"
Because summer vacation is
Just around the corner
Where the school bus never comes.

May 1996

Special Things

Isn't it special
How Jamie knows when
I am just a little bit
Too sad?
He is my brother, and
He loves me forever.
And when
I am just a little bit
Too sad,
He sends me
A rainbow to look at,
Or a butterfly to run with,
Or a feather to catch.
And sometimes,
He sends me
All of those things
Even when I am not so sad.
He just wants me to
Be even happier.

August 1994

On Being a Good Brother

Some day,
I want to tie Jamie's
Brown moose pants
Onto the end of a balloon,
And send them up to Heaven for him.
Don't you think
That would make him happy?
And it would make all the other
Heaven Angels and Children happy, too!
Some day,
We need to do that
Special thing,
Because I want to be a good brother.
I want to do things
That make my Jamie happy.

October 1995

When I Die (Part II)

When I die, I want to be
A child in Heaven.
I want to be
A ten-year-old cherub.
I want to be
A hero in Heaven,
And a peacemaker,
Just like my goal on earth.
I will ask God if I can
Help the people in purgatory.
I will help them think,
About their life,
About their spirits,
About their future.
I will help them
Hear their Heartsongs again,
So they can finally
See the face of God,
So soon.
When I die,
I want to be,
Just like I want to be
Here on earth.

November 1999

I Could... If They Would

If they would find a cure when I'm a kid...
I could ride a bike and sail on rollerblades, and
I could go on really long nature hikes.
If they would find a cure when I'm a teenager...
I could earn my license and drive a car, and
I could dance every dance at my senior prom.
If they would find a cure when I'm a young adult...
I could travel around the world and teach peace, and
I could marry and have children of my own.
If they would find a cure when I'm grown old...
I could visit exotic places and appreciate culture, and
I could proudly share pictures of my grandchildren.
If they would find a cure when I'm alive...
I could live each day without pain and machines, and
I could celebrate the biggest thank you of life ever.
If they would find a cure when I'm buried into Heaven,
I could still celebrate with my brothers and sister there, and
I could still be happy knowing that I was a part of the effort.

June 2000

Meditation: The Wind in My Heart

This is not a dream.
This is real.
I talk with God, and
Even if my eyes are closed,
I am awake, and I know.
Whichever direction
The wind is blowing,
I follow it.
And when the wind stops,
I stop where it stops,
And I see God.
Sometimes,
God looks like a golden harp
That is shaped like a silver flower.
We talk together about health, and
We talk about how babies
And other people die.
Then I hug and kiss God.
I can do that because
God is every-shape.
Every shape that the world has.

He is a circle, a triangle, every-shape.
He is even invisible.
And, He is even human.
So, we can hug God,
If we know how.
I understand, so I hug Him.
God is everywhere the wind takes me.
The wind takes me to God, and
God takes the wind to me.
It asks me where I want to go
Without even saying anything, anyword.
It just knows.
It just knows.
I always see in the wind,
And so, I will follow the wind as it
Moves inside my world and
Inside my house and inside my heart.
I will trust the wind, and
I will let it take me wherever it is going,
Because God is in the wind.
God is the wind,
And I am here for God.

August 1996

December Prayer

No matter who you are,
Say a prayer this season.
No matter what your faith,
Say a prayer this season.
No matter how you celebrate,
Say a prayer this season.
There are so many ways
To celebrate faiths,
There are so many faiths
To celebrate life.
No matter who,
No matter what,
No matter how...
You pray.
Let's say a prayer
This season,
Together, for peace.

December 1999

On Being Thankful

Dear God,
I was going to thank You tonight
For a beautiful sunrise,
That was pink behind the fog down the hill,
And for a wonderful rainbow,
That I ran under pointing to
All my favorite colors,
And for such a great sunset,
That sparkled orange across the water.
I was going to thank You tonight
For all of these special gifts,
Except that none of them happened.
But do You know what?
I still love You, God,
And I have lots of other things
That I can thank You for tonight,
Even if You didn't give those
Very special gifts to me today.
It's okay, God,
Because I'll look for them all again,
When my tomorrow comes.
Amen.

November 1995

The Mattie Book

Sometimes,
I wish I could be in a book.
And the book would have
Lots and lots of pages.
When everyone reads it,
They would know
About Jamie, and Katie and Stevie.
They would know
About God and life,
And about love and Heaven
And about playing and feelings
And rainbows and feathers and
Mommies and peacemakers and
Dinosaurs and friends
And all the other important things.
And all of the pages would
Have lots and lots of words, filled with
Mattie's thoughts and Heartsongs.
And they would live and teach
Saying "Hooray for Life!" forever,
Even after I am gone.

November 1994

A New Hope

I need a hope... a new hope.
A hope that reaches for the stars, and
That does not end in violence or war.
A hope that makes peace on our earth, and
That does not create evil in the world.
A hope that finds cures for all diseases, and
That does not make people hurt,
In their bodies, in their hearts,
Or most of all, in their spirits.
I need a hope... a new hope,
A hope that inspires me to live, and
To make all these things happen,
So that the whole world can have
A new hope, too.

May 1999

61

Eternal Echoes

Our life is an echo
Of our spirit today,
Of our essence
As it is,
Caught between
Our yesterday
And our tomorrow.
It is the resounding
Reality of who we are,
As a result of
Where we have been,
And where we will be,
For eternity.

Spring 2000

About the Author (Part II)

Eleven-year-old Matthew Joseph Thaddeus Stepanek, best known as "Mattie," has been writing poetry and short stories since age three. Mattie's poems have been published in a variety of mediums and he has been an invited speaker for several seminars, conferences and television shows. In 1999, he was awarded the Melinda Lawrence International Book Award for inspirational written works by the Children's Hospice International. He has appeared on *Oprah*, *The Today Show*, *Good Morning America* and many other programs. In addition to writing, Mattie enjoys reading, collecting rocks and shells, and playing with Legos. He has earned a black belt in martial arts, and in 2001, Mattie served as the Maryland State Goodwill Ambassador for the Muscular Dystrophy Association. In 2002, he will serve as both the National Ambassador and the State Ambassador for the MDA. He lives with his mother, Jeni, in Upper Marlboro, MD, where he is home-schooled.

Index

(continued)

Heart Songs

Written and Illustrated by Matthew Joseph Thaddeus Stepanek
"Mattie"

VSP Books

HYPERION

New York

CONTENTS

Senses

Seasons

Celebrations

Sounds of Childhood

Eight New Poems

<u>Dedication</u>
This book is dedicated to those who believe in celebrating the gifts of life every day, especially my mom, all of my kin, and the entire staff of the Pediatric Intensive Care Unit at Children's National Medical Center. Always remember to play after every storm!

Mattie

Stevie

Katie

Jamie

Senses

5

Making Real Sense of the Senses

Our eyes are for looking at things,
But they are also for crying
When we are very happy or very sad.
Our ears are for listening,
But so are our hearts.
Our noses are for smelling food,
But also the wind and the grass and
If we try very hard, butterflies.
Our hands are for feeling,
But also for hugging and touching so gently.
Our mouths and tongues are for tasting,
But also for saying words, like
"I love you," and
"Thank you, God, for all of these things."

The Gift of Color

Thank You
For all the colors of the rainbow.
Thank You
For sharing these colors
With all of the fish
And all of the birds
And all of the flowers
That You have given us.
And thank You
For the colors of the
Heaven-in-the-earth
And of the
Heaven-in-the-sky,
And for sharing these colors
In the people of the world.
You give us color
As a gift, God,
And I thank You
For all of these
Beautiful colors and
Beautiful things and
Beautiful people.
What special gifts
You have given to us!

The Smell of a Noise

Shhhh...
I smell something.
It smells like a noise.
Like a turtle noise.
Yes, that's what it is.
It is a turtle noise,
And it is wonderful,
Because turtles
Live inside of seashells.
Would you like to
Live in a seashell?
It would smell like
A turtle noise,
But I think
It would be wonderful!

Angel-Wings

This morning,
I smelled something very good.
Perhaps,
It was a rainbow.
Or maybe,
It was a dinosaur smile.
Or even,
A seashell.
I am not sure
What I smelled.
And I am not sure
What rainbows
Or dinosaur smiles
Or seashells
Smell like.
But I'm sure they smell wonderful.
Wonderful and special
Like the smell of
Angel-Wings.
But also,
I'm sure they smell
A little sad,
Because we can't really smell
A rainbow,
Or a dinosaur smile,
Or a seashell,
Or especially,
We can't really smell
The wonderful smell
Of Angel-Wings.

Very Special Candy

One day,
I will make a bag of
Very Special Candy.
The candy will come in
All different colors,
Colors like you see in
Good Ordinary Candy.
But...
The flavors will be
So different and
So special and
So wonderful.
There will be little
Blue candies
That taste like sky.
And the little
Green and brown candies
Will taste like grass and trees.
The orange ones
Will taste like butterfly,
The yellow ones
Like flowers and sunshine,
And the white ones
Like clouds in Heaven.
And then,
I will make a very, very
Special piece of candy,
That is all different colors
And that glows like a halo.
And that will be the one
That tastes like
Rainbow and Angels.

When My Feet Itch

When my feet itch,
Maybe I'll think about
Riding on a dinosaur
With my mom —
And then,
I won't remember that my feet itch.
When my feet itch,
Maybe I'll think about
Spending the night at the
North Pole with Santa Claus —
And then,
It will be too cold for my feet to itch.
When my feet itch,
Maybe I'll think about
Playing with Nick and Ben
Because they're some of the
Best friends a kid could ever have —
And then,
I won't care if my feet itch or not.
Or maybe, when my feet itch,
I'll think about Angels —
Because they don't make
You itch when you touch them.

Seasons 12

Leaf for a Day

Today,
I think I will be a tree.
Or perhaps,
A leaf on a branch on the tree.
I will feel
The gentle breeze,
And then I will
`Plip' off of my branch and my tree
And float in the wind.
I will go
Back and forth in the breeze
All the way down to the ground.
And after I rest
And say `hello'
To the grass and dirt and bugs,
I will call to the wind,
`Come and take me
To visit my other leaf-friends
On all of the other trees, please.'
And the gentle breeze
Will come
And pick me up
So that I can jump and dance
With all of the other
Tree-stars and tree-flowers
That God gave the world.
What a special idea
To be, today.

On the Mountain of Tree-Stars

Summer is almost over.
Soon, it will be September,
And then, it will be fall.
And when it is fall,
We can play with all
The tree-stars that fall
To us from up high.
And when the tree-stars fall
From the sky,
We can build a leaf-mountain.
First, when all
The leaves fall
From the sky,
We put them all
Together into a mountain-pile
Way up high.
Then, we get a string and tie
Them all
Together so that when
The wind blows they won't fly
Away from the mountain-pile.
And last, we climb
Up the leaf-mountain,
And we stand up so high
Next to the sky,
And then —- sliiiiiiide —-
We slide
Aaaaaaaalll
The way to the bottom of the mountain-leaf pile.
So when the fall
Comes it will get chilly,
And things will start to fall
Like the season.
But they don't fall
With a boom!
Only they fall
Like a floating leaf, or
Like a little boy on
The Mountain of Tree-Stars.

Winter Luck

Snowflakes...
They come down so slow,
And sometimes so fast,
Looking like pretty stars
Falling down, down, down
To the ground.
Little stars with little holes,
Bigger stars with bigger holes,
They are all cuddly snowflake stars.
Snowflakes of the tiny snows,
Snowstars of the bigger snows,
I will catch you on my hand
Or on my tongue
And make a wish...
I will make a wish on
My falling snowstar,
And then have good luck
All day, all night, all Ever.

Important Things

When I grow up,
I think maybe
I will be a snowman,
Because when it
Snows outside,
I'll already be cold
And like it.
And children will
Play with me,
And laugh
And sing
And dance
All around me.
And those are important
Things to have happen
When you grow up.

16

Indian Winter

Hey!
It's cold out here today!
This is May,
And it's supposed to be
Spring
Turning into
Summer,
So I can have my birthday.
But I need my jacket,
And my hat.
Oh, bother!
I wonder —-
Who played with the seasons
Last night
While we were all sleeping?

The Eye of the Beholder

Dandelions are NOT weeds!
See?
They have beautiful
Yellow flowers on them.
They have lovely
Green stems.
Mommy puts them
In a jar of water
In the kitchen —-
They are flowers!
See?
They are round.
They are round and yellow.
Oh, mommy,
Please tell him
He's making a big mistake!
Poor little dandelions...
He's pulling them all up
And calling them "weeds."
Oh, this is
So horrible, so sad!
What would God say if
He saw you sending all of these
Poor, little, round, yellow
Dandelion-flowers
Back to the Lord?

Summer 'Rememberies'

After everyone has
A smoky cookout at Chip's house,
And the grown-ups make
Music on their guitars for singing and dancing,
And the children take
Off their shoes and run
Around the backyard catching
Lightning bugs in the dark —-
Then, it is a very good time to be
Happy.
And that `then' is
A very good time and
A very good feeling to remember
Ever-after.

Celebrations 20

The Importance of Windows

Windows are very good things to have.
They let you look out,
And see all the different things.
And they let you look in,
To see all the other different things.
And do you know what is the most
Special window of all?
The window in your heart,
That's between the Heaven-in-the-earth,
And the Heaven-in-the-sky.

Circle of Happiness

I am a little kid
For you to love.
I am a little kid
For you to hug and kiss.
I am a little kid
For you to say,
"You are so special,
Yes you are" to.
I am a little kid
For all of those things
And more.
And when you
Feel and say and do
All of those things,
I will be a little kid
Who will love you.
I will be a little kid
Who will hug and kiss you.
I will be a little kid
Who will say to you,
"You are so special, too,
Yes you are."
I will be a little kid
Who will do all of those things
And more.
And that is what
Happiness
Is all about.

On Being Thankful

Dear God,
I was going to thank You tonight
For a beautiful sunrise,
That was pink behind the fog down the hill,
And for a wonderful rainbow,
That I ran under pointing to
All my favorite colors,
And for such a great sunset,
That sparkled orange across the water.
I was going to thank You tonight
For all of these special gifts,
Except that none of them happened.
But do You know what?
I still love You, God,
And I have lots of other things
That I can thank You for tonight,
Even if you didn't give those
Very special gifts to me today.
It's okay, God,
Because I'll look for them all again,
When my tomorrow comes.
Amen.

Pinch of Peace

Dear God,
Tonight my prayers are for the world.
We have to stop this fighting.
We have to stop the wars.
People need to lay down their weapons,
And find peace in their hearts.
People need to stop arguing and hating.
People need to notice the good things.
People need to remember You, God.
Maybe You could come and
Shoot a little bow-and-arrow pinch
Into all the angry peoples' hearts, God.
Then they would feel You again.
And then they would realize what
They are doing and how horrible the
Killing and hating and fighting is,
And they might even begin to pray.
Then, they could reach in, and
Pull the little bow-and-arrow pinch
Out of their hearts and feel good
And be loving and living people again.
And then,
The world would be at peace, and
The children would be safe, and
The people would be happy, and
We could all say "thank You" together.
Amen.

Heartsong

I have a song, deep in my heart,
And only I can hear it.
If I close my eyes and sit very still
It is so easy to listen to my song.
When my eyes are open and
I am so busy and moving and busy,
If I take time and listen very hard,
I can still hear my Heartsong.
It makes me feel happy.
Happier than ever.
Happier than everywhere
And everything and everyone
In the whole wide world.
Happy like thinking about
Going to Heaven when I die.
My Heartsong sounds like this —-
    I love you! I love you!
    How happy you can be!
    How happy you can make
    This whole world be!
And sometimes it's other
Tunes and words, too,
But it always sings the
Same special feeling to me.
It makes me think of
Jamie, and Katie and Stevie,
And other wonderful things.
This is my special song.
But do you know what?
All people have a special song
Inside their hearts!
Everyone in the whole wide world
Has a special Heartsong.
If you believe in magical, musical hearts,
And if you believe you can be happy,
Then you, too, will hear your song.

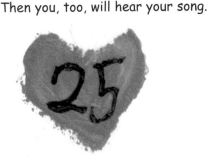

The Daily Gift

You know what?
Tomorrow is a new day.
And today is a new day.
Actually,
Every day is a new day.
Thank You, God,
For all of these
Special and new days.

Special Section—
Eight Additional Poems

Barney-Muffins

Good morning!
It's a smiley-face morning.
Mommy made banana-muffins,
Because it's Stevie's birthday.
I had banana-muffins before,
At Sandy's house.
They were very, very good.
Mommy said these banana-muffins
Taste good, too,
But they are not Real
Because she didn't scratch them,
Like Sandy did.
Hey...
Are these plastic banana-muffins?
I guess we'll just have to
Use our imaginations,
And pretend.

Magical Big-Boy Underpants

Some of my big-boy underpants
Have Mickey Mouse on them.
Some of my big-boy underpants
Have Barney on them.
But some of my big-boy underpants
Are just white.
Maybe, the white underpants
Could be like
The trees in the fall,
And turn into colors.
They could change into orange
And red and yellow.
And they would be beautiful,
And very special,
And I would wear them and
Be very happy.
Except I wouldn't be happy
If they fell down,
Like the leaves do,
Onto the ground.
Then, I would get cold,
And I might trip and
Fall down, too.

Morning Shoes

Listen...
Listen carefully to the people
When they are walking to work,
Or to school, or to play,
Or even to wherever,
And the shoes can tell you what
Kind of breakfast cereal their people eat.
The ladies hurrying in pointy high-heels eat
  Coco-coco-coco-poppin'
  Coco-coco-coco-poppin'...
The men with boots and heavy steps eat
  Crunchabooma-crunchabooma-
  Crunchabooma-crunchabooma...
The teenagers who forget to tie their sneakers eat
  Sugar-chewy-munchy-boomy
  Sugar-chewy-munchy-boomy...
The children in sandals and Velcro shoes eat
  Twinkle-crinkle-marshmallow sprinkle,
  Twinkle-crinkle-marshmallow sprinkle...
And the old man in his bedroom slippers at the bus stop eats
  Snap-crackle-rustle pop,
  Snap-crackle-rustle pop...
But the babies in their strollers with little soft shoes
That have no dirt marks on the bottoms of them
Don't make any noise at all...
That's because they eat oatmeal,
And listen to hear what the grown-ups eat
So they know what to ask for when they get older.

Where the Earth Stops

Do you know where the earth stops
And it's the end of it?
It can be when you come to water,
But not usually.
Do you know why?
Because if you go out of earth
And you don't have a rocket ship
With you and you're not driving one,
You will come to the end of the earth
When you go into space.
It will be a long way,
But you can make it.
Have fun on your trip,
Bye!

The Storm

There is a big storm coming.
It is way up in the air,
Above the clouds.
It is out in space.
Maybe my friends and I
Will get into a rocket ship
And fly up into space
To see the storm.
We will look down at the storm.
When the storm is all through,
We will come back down to earth.
We will be dry, not wet,
Because we were above the storm clouds.
But it will take a long time
To fly up into that space.
So maybe,
If it is snack time,
Perhaps we will just use
An umbrella to stay dry instead.

<u>Evening Thought</u>

When it is getting
To be nighttime,
But it is
Not dark yet,
The farm animals
Begin to get very tired.
They need to go
Into their barns,
And inside their stables,
And inside their hutches,
And homes,
So that when
The pink and gray sunset
Is all finished,
They can go
Right to sleep,
And have
Pleasant dreams.

Scrub-a-Dub

Help, help!
All I did was take a bath!
A long bubble bath.
I washed my face,
And my hands and my feet.
I played with my mermaid,
And my whale and my boat.
And now,
Now I have
Raisin-fingers and raisin-toes!
Oh no!
Help, help!
I guess I better
Get back into the bathtub,
And wash away these
Raisin-hands and raisin-feet!
And since I am in there,
I guess I better
Just play some more,
Don't you know?

Night-Light Magic

Last night,
My mommy forgot
To turn on my night-light.
I was scared,
So I called her.
Mommy turned on the light,
And then she kissed me,
And tucked me in again.
And then,
I was a golden head in the night.
That is when I'm a little boy,
Between an Angel,
And a Wild Thing.

Index

The publishers wish to acknowledge the assistance and support of the following people in the production of this book: Martha Shaw Whitley, our amazing sister, for organizing and coordinating the people and events which allow Mattie's book to be shared far and wide; Marissa L. Garis, public relations and marketing specialist at Children's National Medical Center for introducing us to Mattie and his mom, Jeni, and giving us the opportunity to publish Mattie's poems; Catherine Morrison, our production director, who tries to keep us all organized; and Jeni Stepanek, Mattie's mom, whose hidden talents as an editor are greatly appreciated.

Peter and Cheryl Barnes
VSP Books
Alexandria, Virginia
June 2001

Write Your Own
Heartsongs

Write Your Own
Heartsongs

Write Your Own
Heartsongs

Write Your Own Heartsongs